Baby, the Poodle Cow Dog

Inspired by a true story

Story by Willyn Webb Illustrations by Denise Theobald

WESTERN REFLECTIONS PUBLISHING COMPANY®
Lake City, CO

Dedicated in loving memory to the one and only "Mom" with special thanks to David Smith for his patience, prayers, and wisdom.

ISBN 978-1-932738-40-7

Library of Congress Control Number: 2006940425

First Edition
Printed in China

Western Reflections Publishing Company®
P.O. Box 1149, 951 N. Highway 149
Lake City, CO 81235
1-800-993-4490
www.westernreflectionspub.com

Hello from the Author!

Have you ever felt too little, too afraid, or too out-of-place to even try? Well, the story you are about to read is true, and it may change your mind about trying. It is about my daughter and her pet poodle who, with a big dose of faith and determination, proved the grownups in their lives wrong. It tells how Baby the poodle became Baby the cow dog right before our very amazed eyes.

As you read, look for Baby in the photographs and drawings that tell the story. He is very small and does not seem to fit in. But he is proof that with desire and effort even the biggest and most unlikely dreams can come true.

Some of the words in this story may be unfamiliar to you. The meaning of the words in bold print can be found in the glossary at the back of the book.

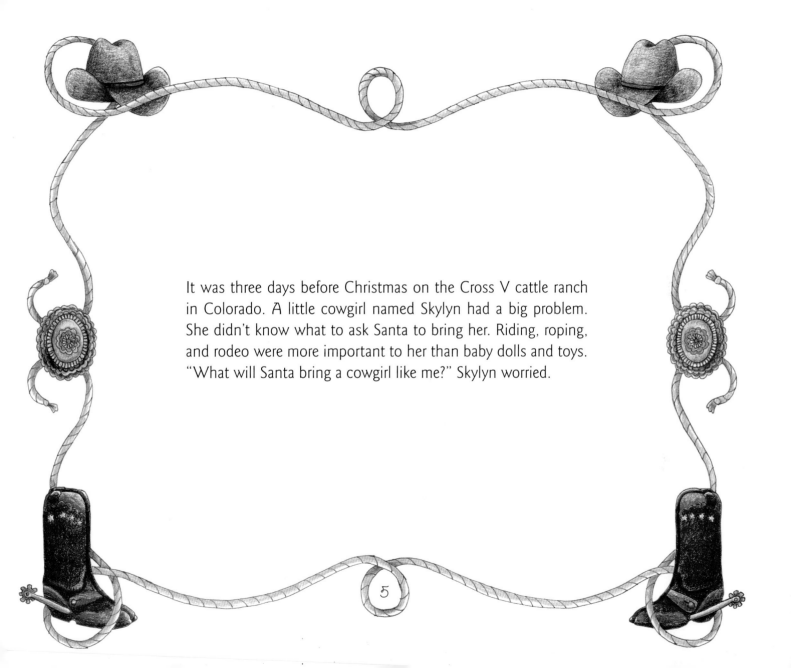

It was three days before Christmas on the Cross V cattle ranch in Colorado. A little cowgirl named Skylyn had a big problem. She didn't know what to ask Santa to bring her. Riding, roping, and rodeo were more important to her than baby dolls and toys. "What will Santa bring a cowgirl like me?" Skylyn worried.

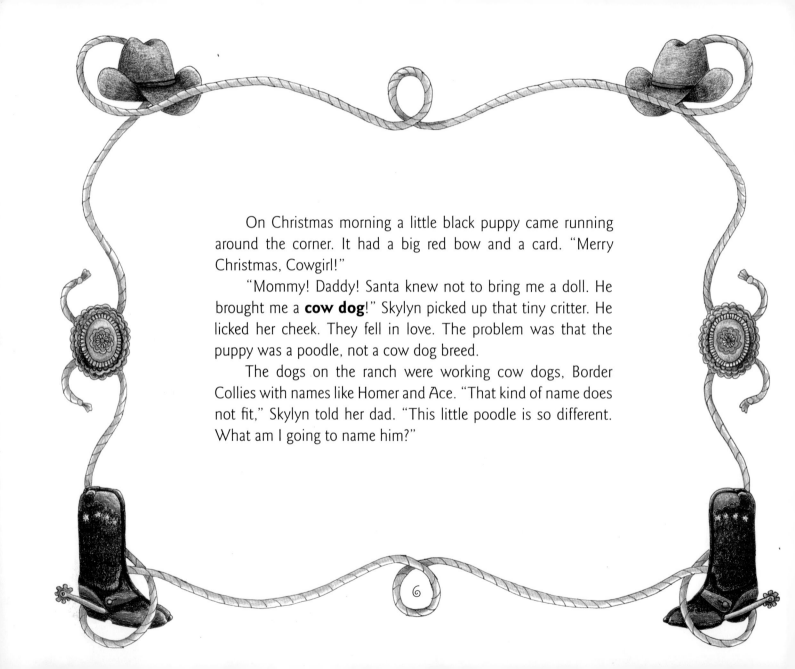

On Christmas morning a little black puppy came running around the corner. It had a big red bow and a card. "Merry Christmas, Cowgirl!"

"Mommy! Daddy! Santa knew not to bring me a doll. He brought me a **cow dog**!" Skylyn picked up that tiny critter. He licked her cheek. They fell in love. The problem was that the puppy was a poodle, not a cow dog breed.

The dogs on the ranch were working cow dogs, Border Collies with names like Homer and Ace. "That kind of name does not fit," Skylyn told her dad. "This little poodle is so different. What am I going to name him?"

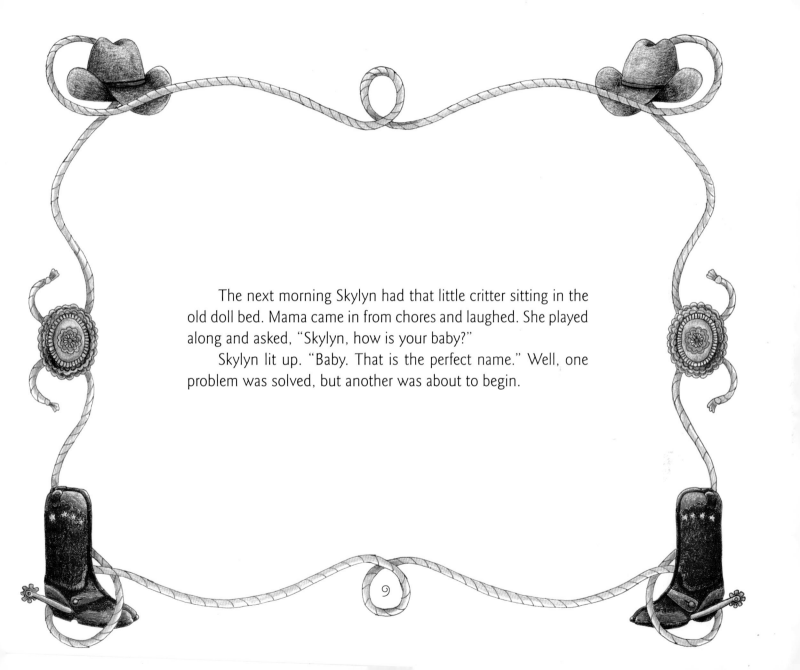

The next morning Skylyn had that little critter sitting in the old doll bed. Mama came in from chores and laughed. She played along and asked, "Skylyn, how is your baby?"

Skylyn lit up. "Baby. That is the perfect name." Well, one problem was solved, but another was about to begin.

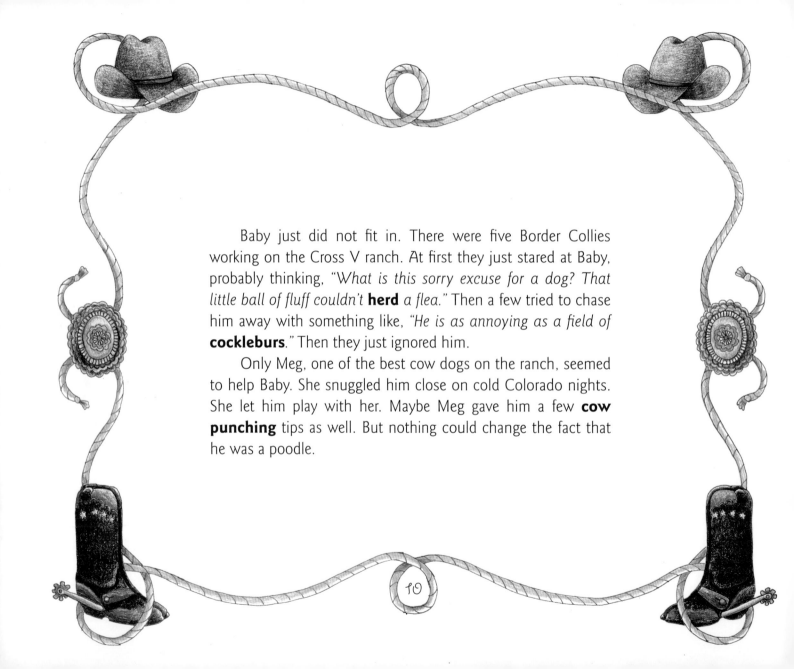

Baby just did not fit in. There were five Border Collies working on the Cross V ranch. At first they just stared at Baby, probably thinking, *"What is this sorry excuse for a dog? That little ball of fluff couldn't* **herd** *a flea."* Then a few tried to chase him away with something like, *"He is as annoying as a field of* **cockleburs***."* Then they just ignored him.

Only Meg, one of the best cow dogs on the ranch, seemed to help Baby. She snuggled him close on cold Colorado nights. She let him play with her. Maybe Meg gave him a few **cow punching** tips as well. But nothing could change the fact that he was a poodle.

Skylyn never planned on taking Baby around the ranch. *"What if a cow kicks? What if my horse sidesteps? It could be dangerous for such a little dog."*

But nothing stopped Baby. That poodle would not let Skylyn **hit the trail** without him. Trotting, loping, or making dust at top speed, he kept up. Somehow Baby always got to the cows. *"Was he trying to prove his name was a mistake?"* All around the ranch Skylyn and Baby helped out. *"Did he think he was a Border Collie, too?"*

Roundup time rolled around. Everyone was excited. Skylyn and her sisters had been riding on the ranch all summer, and they all thought they should get to go. "Mommy, Daddy, Papa, can we go this year?" they begged.

"You are bigger," said her dad, "but Skylyn is the oldest."

Her mom added, "She rides as good as any **hand**."

"Please," said Skylyn.

"It is a long day," said Papa. "But we need all the help we can get. I think Skylyn is ready."

Skylyn cheered, "Yahoo!"

She would be riding on the mountain! Her sisters didn't get to go. That made it even better, but cowboys

and cowgirls from other ranches would be there. Skylyn wondered, *"What would they think of a little cowgirl? Would the real cowboys and cowgirls laugh?"*

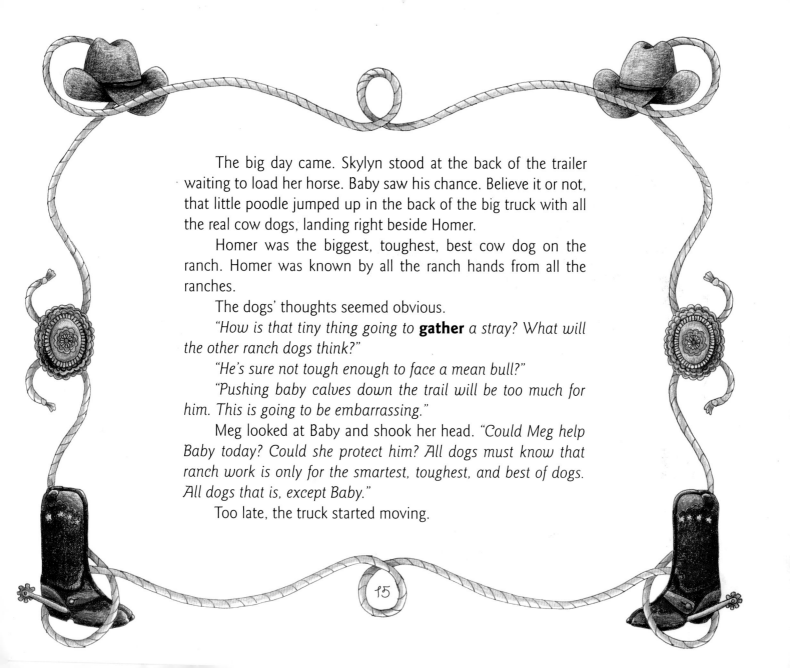

The big day came. Skylyn stood at the back of the trailer waiting to load her horse. Baby saw his chance. Believe it or not, that little poodle jumped up in the back of the big truck with all the real cow dogs, landing right beside Homer.

Homer was the biggest, toughest, best cow dog on the ranch. Homer was known by all the ranch hands from all the ranches.

The dogs' thoughts seemed obvious.

"How is that tiny thing going to **gather** *a stray? What will the other ranch dogs think?"*

"He's sure not tough enough to face a mean bull?"

"Pushing baby calves down the trail will be too much for him. This is going to be embarrassing."

Meg looked at Baby and shook her head. *"Could Meg help Baby today? Could she protect him? All dogs must know that ranch work is only for the smartest, toughest, and best of dogs. All dogs that is, except Baby."*

Too late, the truck started moving.

Papa, the owner and cow boss, drove the Cross V crew to the **summer range**. It was on top of Grand Mesa. Skylyn usually loved listening to the cowboys and cowgirls talk. But today was different. *"Was she ready? Could she really handle the mountain?"* Her thoughts raced as the truck and trailer slowly climbed the mountain curves.

They were the first ones to arrive. Baby jumped out. Skylyn saw him. "Oh, no, Baby. Not today." Proving yourself a real hand to the cowboys and cowgirls on the mountain was hard. "I'm ready to give it a go. But can you do it too?" Skylyn asked Baby. Then she asked herself, *"Will he even be safe?"*

He wagged that little tail. "You and I are becoming true cow hands. Aren't we? Even if we don't look like it. We are." Baby was okay at home, but the real test was on the mountain. Today.

Papa was sitting on his big black horse when he spotted Baby. "How did he get here?" Papa looked worried.

Skylyn took a deep breath. "Papa, can Baby go on the roundup too?"

"It is dangerous," Papa warned.

Skylyn explained, "He is really tough."

"What if he gets in the way?" Papa questioned.

"He can help," Skylyn said with confidence.

Papa did not want any trouble for Skylyn. "This is going to be a big day for you. Are you sure you want to mess with that poodle?"

"I am sure," Skylyn said.

Papa replied, "Ok. We are **burning daylight**."

It was time.

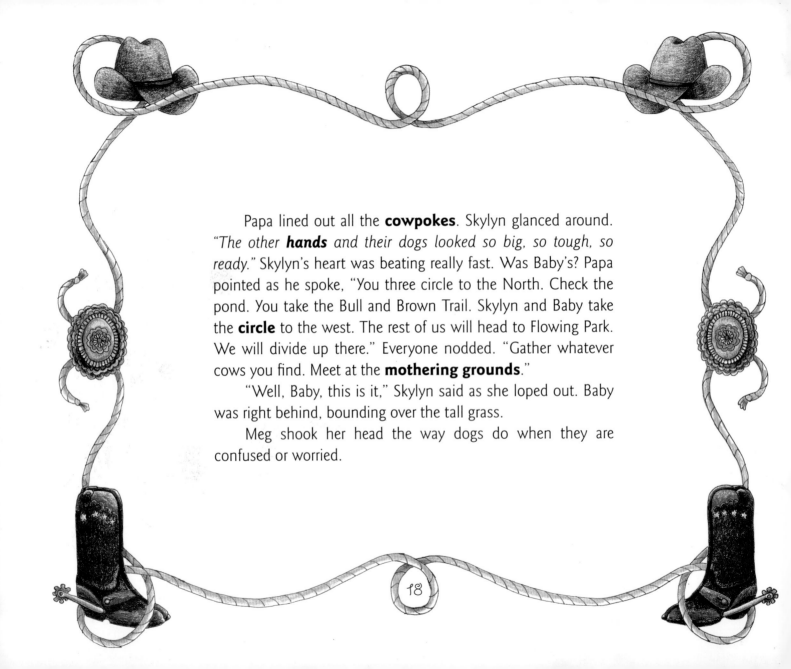

Papa lined out all the **cowpokes**. Skylyn glanced around. *"The other **hands** and their dogs looked so big, so tough, so ready."* Skylyn's heart was beating really fast. Was Baby's? Papa pointed as he spoke, "You three circle to the North. Check the pond. You take the Bull and Brown Trail. Skylyn and Baby take the **circle** to the west. The rest of us will head to Flowing Park. We will divide up there." Everyone nodded. "Gather whatever cows you find. Meet at the **mothering grounds**."

"Well, Baby, this is it," Skylyn said as she loped out. Baby was right behind, bounding over the tall grass.

Meg shook her head the way dogs do when they are confused or worried.

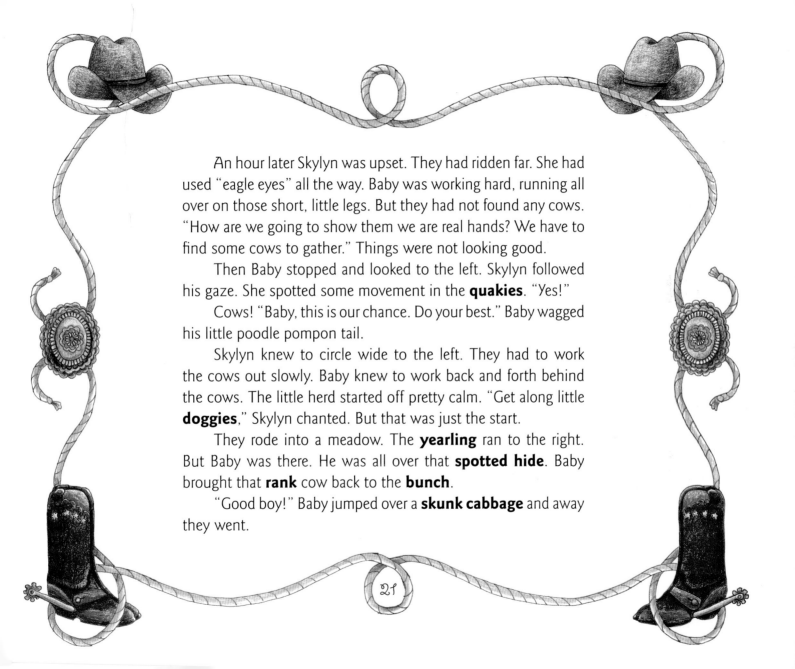

An hour later Skylyn was upset. They had ridden far. She had used "eagle eyes" all the way. Baby was working hard, running all over on those short, little legs. But they had not found any cows. "How are we going to show them we are real hands? We have to find some cows to gather." Things were not looking good.

Then Baby stopped and looked to the left. Skylyn followed his gaze. She spotted some movement in the **quakies**. "Yes!"

Cows! "Baby, this is our chance. Do your best." Baby wagged his little poodle pompon tail.

Skylyn knew to circle wide to the left. They had to work the cows out slowly. Baby knew to work back and forth behind the cows. The little herd started off pretty calm. "Get along little **doggies**," Skylyn chanted. But that was just the start.

They rode into a meadow. The **yearling** ran to the right. But Baby was there. He was all over that **spotted hide**. Baby brought that **rank** cow back to the **bunch**.

"Good boy!" Baby jumped over a **skunk cabbage** and away they went.

It seemed like hours, days, weeks. Often a cow would head in the wrong direction. Skylyn would go out and around the cow to bring it back. At the same time a cow on the other side would take off. Back and forth she went. Back and forth went Baby. It was hard work, but on they trod.

They had to get them all to the mothering grounds. There was not a clear trail. It was very rocky. Baby must be getting tired. *"Stay calm. Be cowgirl tough,"* Skylyn told herself. Baby looked at her. He must have heard the worry in her voice. Skylyn looked at Baby. "We can do it. We are true cowhands."

"I said it, but do I believe it?" she asked herself.

Meanwhile, back at the mothering grounds the cowboys were holding a rowdy bunch of about 300 **head** of cows. Homer and Meg were pacing back and forth. Were they worried about Baby? Skylyn and Baby should be back by now. Mama said a little prayer.

It was a loud place. Mother cows were calling their calves. The baby calves were calling their mamas. Papa was watching. *"Where were Skylyn and Baby?"*

Someone yelled. It was a couple cowpokes from the other ranch coming in with a little bunch. It was good they were all there because...

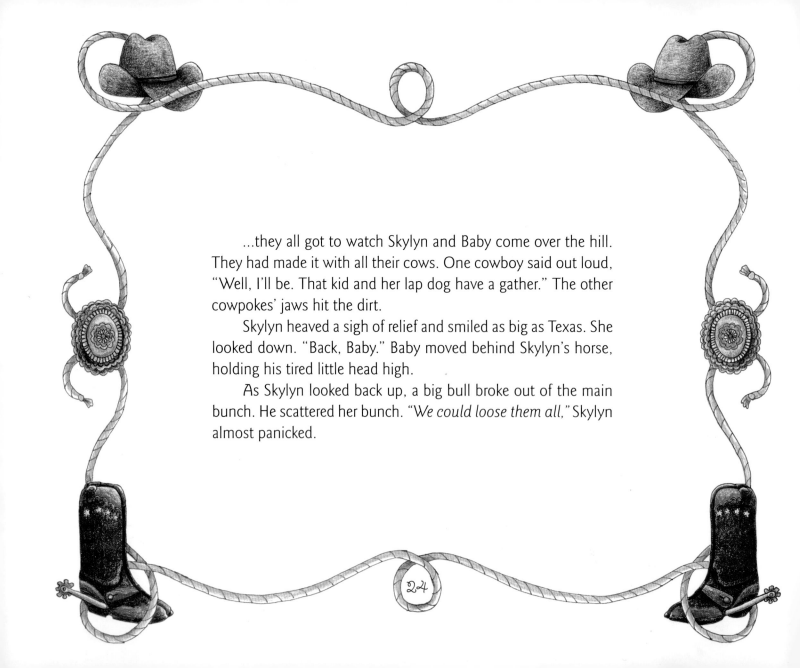

...they all got to watch Skylyn and Baby come over the hill. They had made it with all their cows. One cowboy said out loud, "Well, I'll be. That kid and her lap dog have a gather." The other cowpokes' jaws hit the dirt.

Skylyn heaved a sigh of relief and smiled as big as Texas. She looked down. "Back, Baby." Baby moved behind Skylyn's horse, holding his tired little head high.

As Skylyn looked back up, a big bull broke out of the main bunch. He scattered her bunch. *"We could loose them all,"* Skylyn almost panicked.

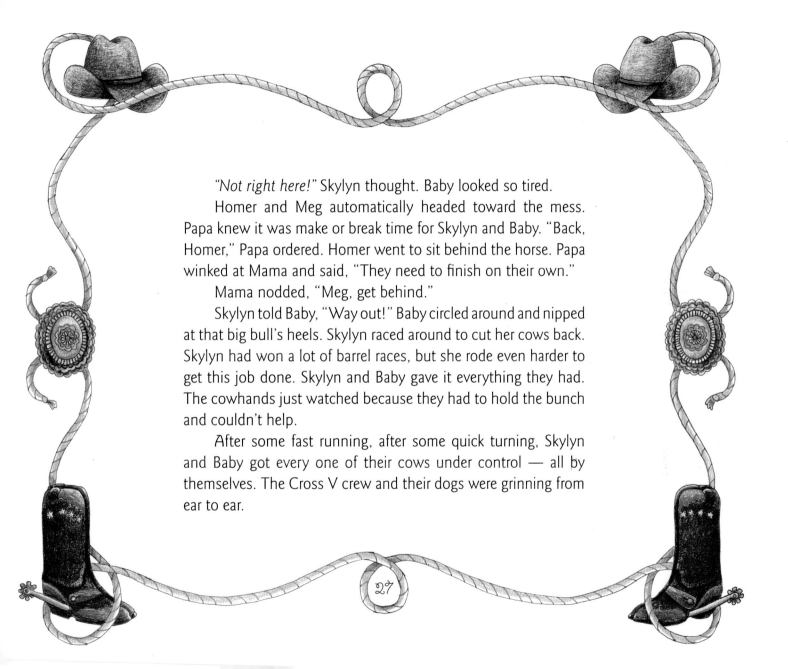

"Not right here!" Skylyn thought. Baby looked so tired.

Homer and Meg automatically headed toward the mess. Papa knew it was make or break time for Skylyn and Baby. "Back, Homer," Papa ordered. Homer went to sit behind the horse. Papa winked at Mama and said, "They need to finish on their own."

Mama nodded, "Meg, get behind."

Skylyn told Baby, "Way out!" Baby circled around and nipped at that big bull's heels. Skylyn raced around to cut her cows back. Skylyn had won a lot of barrel races, but she rode even harder to get this job done. Skylyn and Baby gave it everything they had. The cowhands just watched because they had to hold the bunch and couldn't help.

After some fast running, after some quick turning, Skylyn and Baby got every one of their cows under control — all by themselves. The Cross V crew and their dogs were grinning from ear to ear.

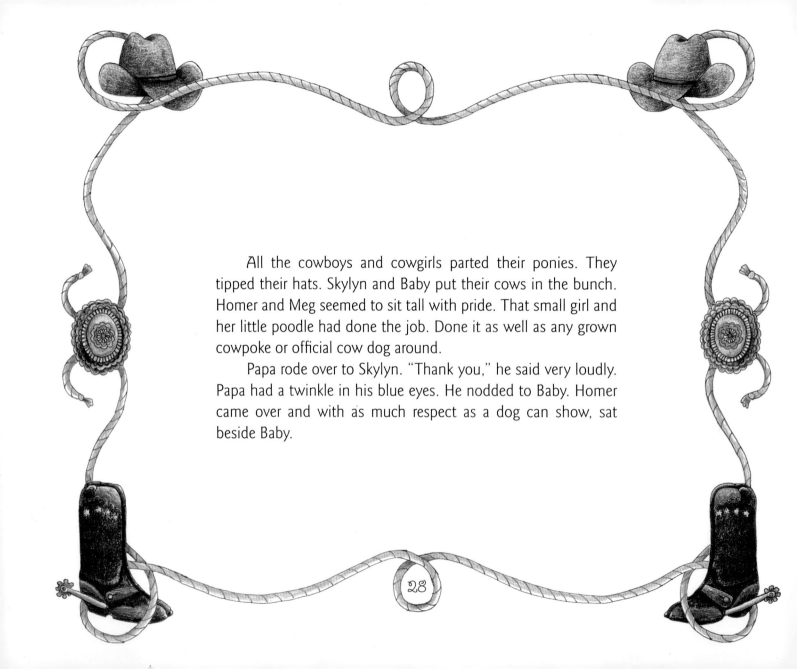

All the cowboys and cowgirls parted their ponies. They tipped their hats. Skylyn and Baby put their cows in the bunch. Homer and Meg seemed to sit tall with pride. That small girl and her little poodle had done the job. Done it as well as any grown cowpoke or official cow dog around.

Papa rode over to Skylyn. "Thank you," he said very loudly. Papa had a twinkle in his blue eyes. He nodded to Baby. Homer came over and with as much respect as a dog can show, sat beside Baby.

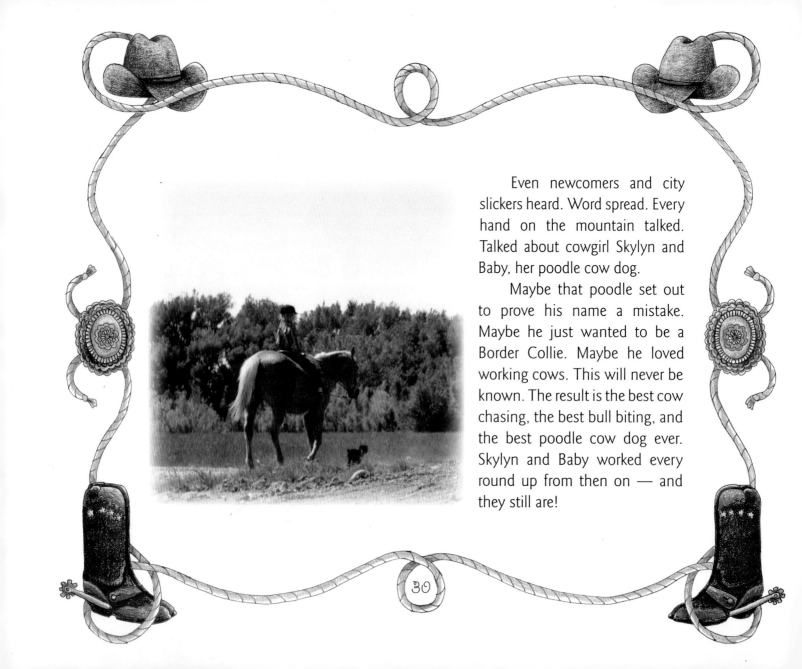

Even newcomers and city slickers heard. Word spread. Every hand on the mountain talked. Talked about cowgirl Skylyn and Baby, her poodle cow dog.

Maybe that poodle set out to prove his name a mistake. Maybe he just wanted to be a Border Collie. Maybe he loved working cows. This will never be known. The result is the best cow chasing, the best bull biting, and the best poodle cow dog ever. Skylyn and Baby worked every round up from then on — and they still are!

GLOSSARY

bunch: (n.) a group of cows all standing together (v.) to put cows together in a group.

burning daylight: wasting time.

circle: (n.) a route to look at a specific area of land (v.) to move your horse in a circle around a cow to turn it in another direction.

cow dog: a dog trained to herd cattle and work on a ranch.

cowhand (hand), cowpoke, cow puncher: a person that works on a cattle ranch.

cockleburs: weed that has round, pointed burrs on it. The burrs stick in animals' fur and irritates them.

doggies: cowboy term for baby calves or cows.

gather: (n.) a group of cows a cowboy or cowgirl finds and brings in to the herd (v.) to surround cows and move them in to the herd.

head: used to say how many cows are in the herd (300 head).

herd: (n.) a group of cows and calves. (v.) to keep or move animals together.

hit the trail: get moving.

mothering grounds: a grassy meadow where the mother cows find their calves after being mixed up during the cattle drive.

quakies: Aspen trees.

rank: mean or wild cow.

roundup: gathering all of the cows in an large area together in a group.

skunk cabbage: a plant that grows in the mountains of Colorado.

spotted hide: a cow with spots on its hide.

summer range: the mountain pastures where cows graze in the summer.

yearling: year old calf.

Goodbye from the Author!

Wow! Baby and Skylyn did what they set out to do. Was it easy? No. Were they afraid? Yes, sometimes. But, what they accomplished was worth all their hard work.

Now it is your turn. Set a worthy goal and reach it. At the very least, try. As you grow older you will find that your life is a journey from one dream to another. It is all up to you. Enjoy your adventure.